PAY THE PRICE

IT IS WORTH IT

ADAMU DANLAMI

ISBN-9798372230316

DEDICATION

This book is dedicated to my dearly beloved wife in person of Nurse Priscilla for her encouragement and love.

CONTENTS

ACKNOWLEDGMENTS

First and foremost, I want to acknowledge the faithfulness of the Almighty God over my life for his protection provision and inspiration in my life throughout the period of my study particularly the period of coupling this book. Secondly my gratitude and appreciation go to my dearly beloved wife for her Support effort tireless attention and encouragement in making this book a successful One may God bless you abundantly (Amen)

INTRODUCTION

There is a price tag to everything in life, nothing is actually free, we have to pay for what we want in one way or the other. Life is design in such a beautiful way that as human we have to pay the price of making it look actually beautiful in the real life.

What we often get for free, human doesn't really place value on it. When something is gotten for, we don't really know the price tag on it, so we tend to mismanage or use it often.

Dr. Myles Munroe said and I quote "if purpose of a thing is not known abuse is inevitable" that is to say there is a need to always know what we want and how much its cost us to get that, so as to maintained and manage if finally gotten.

There is a need to know and understand the

worth of everything we either want or need, because that is the only way we can actually maintained it. There is a saying; "there's no such thing as a free lunch". Which mean that everything you want in life has a price connected to it. I am not necessarily talking about money. But there is a price to pay if you want to make things better, a price to pay just for leaving things as they are, with other words a price for everything.

I am talking about the very willingness to try to achieve what one wants to achieve. Wishing for something is easy, another thing is to understand that to achieve something, one must set a goal, and be willing to work to reach the goal. To a very large extent, I often see that many do not see or understand the work many put in to be able to succeed in achieving their goals. While others work all their lives without reaching their goals.

It is all about understanding the connection

between wanting something and prioritizing something else. It is about asking yourself the questions is this something I really want? Have I really thought through what I dream of and want? Or is it just an airy thought. Do I really have enough passion for this wish? Am I really ready to re-prioritize things in my life to achieve what I want and dream of?

Let us pretend for just a moment that I had decided to put in the time and effort to learn how to play piano and I got really, good at it. I got so good at it that I ended up as a famous classic musician and touring around the world playing classical piano. I made tons of money, partied with other famous people, stayed in the finest hotels, did not have to clean up after myself, and did not have to cook a meal. This may sound great to you. At the time I made the decision not to learn to play piano, the only "price" I saw was one of time/fun. If it turned out I did not like the piano lessons, I would still have to keep it up for who knows how long. Think about it — Everything has its price. You pay for the choices you make in life.

We can pay for choices we do not make like natural disasters, accidents, etc., and for what we choose not to do for example, getting an education, saving for a rainy day, learning a new thing. Some of the ways in which we pay are with our time, freedom, money, trust, peace of mind, health, relationships, privacy, and tears. No matter what we want of life we must give up something to get it.

CHAPTER ONE

EVERYTHING HAS A PRICE TO PAY

When we want something, we must be willing to pay the cost to achieve it.

You might have heard this sentence- Everything has a Price written on books or the internet or said by your Mathematics teacher who has a secret interest in philosophy.

But have you ever wondered what the real meaning of this sentence is?

We know most commercial objects have a price, but how does everything have a price?

What about the free shirt I got on Buy One Get One offer? What about the free tutorials on YouTube that teaches me various skills? And what about the lovely time I spend with my spouse? They don't charge any money.

Well, they are free, but they aren't free. Forgive me; I know it's getting confusing.

To understand the true meaning, we must first understand what the term everything signifies here.

The term everything not only means the commercial products and services like clothes, gadgets, grocery, stationery, consulting, or digital marketing, but everything we do, feel, sense, achieve or have.

This includes success, happiness, peace of mind, health and fitness, money, sleep, enjoyment, relationships, growth and development, and everything you can think of.

And, all these things have a price which isn't always money. Then what?

Well, according to the situation, the price can be different: effort, hard work, time, attention, consistency, maintaining habits, going through difficult situations, handling stress, suffering pain, etc.

Let's make it more clearly through some examples.

Let's say you got success by landing your dream job. You didn't invest any money for this, but still, the success was not free. How?

Because you had to put months of effort into developing the required skills. You had to gain various experiences, consistently work on your soft skills, build your resume, and prepare for the interview.

You put your time and hard work as a price for getting the job. Hence your success was not free.

In fact, every success comes at a price. You may see someone becoming successful overnight, earning millions within a day, or getting viral on social media and achieving fame.

But do you know how much effort they might have put in before landing in that situation? They may have worked years without any result to see an overnight success suddenly. No success is free.

Let's take another example. Say you are happy with your life because you earn like Elon Musk and have a sweet spouse. You may argue that your happiness is free; it didn't cost you any money.

That's true, happiness is financially free, but there is a price.

You may had to put effort and time into your business and relationship, overcome challenges and suffer pain to get to the point where you earn fascinating money and enjoy a fulfilling relationship.

Similarly, you may be healthy and fit, but you had to discipline yourself to work out every day in the gym and eat fresh vegetables, not McDonald's mouth-watering french fries. Hard work and discipline are the prices.

You may sleep peacefully nowadays, but you achieve this because you drain all your energy every day (that's the price).

You may have got free YouTube tutorials that have helped you build valuable skills, but they show ads and cost your attention. Further development of any skill needs desire and regular efforts.

You may have a good life, but you achieved these by going through bad days.

Everything you have or accomplished has a cost you have paid, or are paying, or will pay. Nothing is free.

Everything you want in life has a price connected to it. There's a price to pay if you want to make things better, a price to pay just for leaving things as they are, a price for everything.

CHAPTER TWO

CONCEPT OF PAYING THE PRICE IN LIFE

Now it's pretty clear that everything has a price. But why do we have to know this? Can we apply this concept in our lives and benefit from it? The answer is an absolute yes!

You might have observed most of the time, the price causes suffering, and the reward we achieve through the price causes happiness. Hence, prices (like hard work) are avoided, and rewards (like success) are favored. But the world is pretty good at keeping balance; it only hands you what you have paid for.

Let's say you have a stable business earning enough money just to pay your bills. You are playing safe.

But you always wanted to be a millionaire. So, you start taking risks and work hard on your business. And suddenly, things begin to get complicated.

The whole universe seems against you. You face failures, criticisms, and business-ruining risks. All the stability you had is gone.

You may think trying to grow your business was a mistake because that's what made everything difficult. And then may give up on your dream.

At this point, if you had realized everything has a price, you might not have given up and increased your chances of success.

You wanted to be a millionaire, right? What do you think, it will happen quickly? You would have a desire, everything will be in your favor and whoosh…. you have millions in your hand. If it happened like this, everyone would be a millionaire.

You have to pay the price. The price is putting effort consistently, solving problems, and suffering all the pain that comes your way. If you pay the required price, you will be rewarded with millions in your hand.

Similarly, if you want happiness, you have to go through struggles. If you want a good relationship, you have to go through fights and bitter moments. If you want fitness, you must ensure some painful gym hours every week.

Whenever you try to achieve a goal, terrible things happen, or you face

problems. At this point, please don't get demotivated and give up. Instead, think of facing those bad situations and solving those problems as a price. The more prices you pay, the closer you get to your target.

Every dream requires a price to make it real. People are not willing to pay the price. That's why their dreams have not become a reality.

Whenever you desire to achieve something, always ask yourselves- am I willing to pay what it requires? If you pay, you will get what you want. Nobody can stop it from happening.

Everything Has a Price- write this sentence in big, bold letters on a page and paste it onto a wall. Read the sentence every day. Let it sink into your mind. It will remind you that all the painful moments are the price you pay for the happiness in life

CHAPTER THREE

SUCCESS OR SACRIFICE

Each and every person needs to succeed at something. Regardless of whether it be sports, school, their activity, or even the general idea of life. Sacrifice some idea of opportunity so as to succeed. Sacrifice is more important than success since one cannot make without sacrificing something first.

Something that everyone wants to achieve is success. Success is not something that comes easy in life, one must be prepared to give sacrifices such as time, in order for them to reach a professional level of success. In order to succeed, people must learn to make sacrifices in life.

Sacrifice is necessary for people to succeed because if people are not willing to sacrifice anything such as time or effort, they will not succeed. They need to sacrifice dedication, effort, and time. These three fundamental principles if used correctly, are the best tools in the race for success. If the rules of using maximum effort, dedication, and time are followed to its highest potential, individuals seeking success will find it. The common, or “magic”, number is 10,000 hours of practice in order for one to become master or professional at what they are trying to accomplish. Most professional athletes such as hockey players have been playing the sport for just about as long as they could walk. For example, most of the skaters on the 18u Syracuse Stars AAA hockey team started playing the game at ages 3,4, or 5. Every player on that team is fundamentally sound when it comes to the game. They have been around it for so long that hockey became a way of life, these are the players, that dedicate the most time in order to succeed. They give the small amount of practice time that they have every day, 100% every time they touch the ice. The hockey players across the world that dedicate the most time to their sport, will be the ones who end up having the best chance at becoming a professional. The same goes for any profession in which one would like to excel in. The hockey coach for the Syracuse Stars 18u AAA team always says "You get out of it, what you put in it boys" (Coach Dan Jones).

Both success and sacrifice go hand in hand, always know that the success worth the sacrifice so pay the price.

CHAPTER FOUR

EVERYTHNG COMES WITH A PRICE

You can never gain something if you don't sacrifice something of equal value. Everything comes with a price.

Everything comes with a price means basically the same thing as Choose your battles. You have to decide if the consequences of an action are worth taking the action. While not everything costs money, everything does have consequences. A similar saying is, "You have to pay the piper if you want to dance."

It is now left for you to identify the price and sacrifice needed to achieve your goals and aspiration in life. There is no man without a purpose

But you see you will have to a pay a price of discovering purpose in life otherwise you will not make a leaving rather you will just be those that have ever existed.

Dr. Myles Munroe said and I quote “the greatest tragedy in life is not death, the greatest tragedy in life is life without a purpose”

Beloved pay the price

Your life can be as good and as excellent as you dream of it.

In the moral and political domains, sacrifice is tied to the idea of self-transcendence, in which an individual sacrifice his or her self-interest for the sake of higher values and commitments. While self-sacrifice has great potential moral value, it can also be used to justify the most brutal acts.

Sacrifice is centered around time. When one sacrifices for something that can reward them in the future, they can put time in their favor. The great thing about sacrifice is that it is temporary. By sacrificing for your goals, you are temporarily giving up one thing, for the long-term success of another thing

ABOUT THE AUTHOR

Adamu Danlami is a graduate of prestigious Federal Polytechnic Bida, Niger state Nigeria. Where he studied Chemistry in Science Laboratory Technology. He is married to Priscilla Jiya, they have no kids yet.

He is from the family of eleven, nine children, first born among them.

Adamu Danlami is a writer and authors of so many books and a graphic designer based in Nigeria.

He is passionate about helping others raise to their full potentials in the area of destiny and purpose in Life.

www.ingramcontent.com/pod-product-compliance
Lightning Source LLC
La Vergne TN
LVHW020545160826
845677LV00015B/4214

* 9 7 9 8 3 7 2 2 3 0 3 1 6 *